I0845669

Tailoring Corporate Social Media Presence

Table of Contents

Your culture is your brand. On social media, people don't just connect with companies, they connect with the people behind the logo.

— Tony Hsieh

Chapter 1. Introduction

In the era of digital connection, sculpting a compelling Corporate Social Media Presence is no longer optional—it's a core part of business strategy. Welcome to our Special Report, an engaging and comprehensive guide, dedicated to arm you with practical insights and proven tactics to tailor your corporate social media presence thoughtfully. This illuminating report is brimming with fascinating case studies, expert interviews, and user-friendly tips that are designed to help you navigate the vibrant social media landscape. Whether you're starting from scratch or redefining your existing presence, this report is your ticket to a more impactful and resonant social media journey. Come, let's ride the wave of digital transformation together, connecting, engaging, and inspiring like never before!

Chapter 2. Understanding the Power of Social Media in Business

As industries progressively transition into the digital space, it becomes contingent upon corporations to comprehend the magnitude and potential of social media's influence over business operations. This in-depth examination divulges the extent of this power and how it can be effectively harnessed to serve a variety of business objectives.

2.1. The Value of Social Media in Today's Digital Landscape

Social media's ubiquity has rendered it a crucial facet of the global digital landscape. It has crossed the threshold of being merely a platform for personal communication and entertainment, evolving into a potent tool for business growth, brand building and customer engagement. With approximately 4.2 billion active users worldwide, the virtual realm presents a colossal audience for businesses to tap into.

To utilize this potential, businesses need to understand what social media brings to the table. With social media, corporations can reach a global audience, forge strong relationships with their consumers, promote real-time interaction, and deliver customer service more efficiently. Furthermore, it paves the way for tapping into consumer data and insights, which serve as a compass to guide business strategies.

2.2. Driving Customer Engagement with Social Media

One major aspect of leveraging social media's power lies in bolstering customer engagement. Social media platforms afford a conversational tone and direct contact with consumers, radiating an aura of personalization around the brand. Businesses can communicate with their audience, gather feedback, and respond to queries in real-time, ultimately nurturing stronger relationships. This interactive nature of social media fosters a sense of community around the brand and helps cement customer loyalty.

Moreover, social media allows corporations to generate and curate tailored content that resonates with their audience, contributing to better brand recall and audience retention. By blending information with entertainment (termed as infotainment), businesses can secure their audience's attention and elicit desired responses.

2.3. Brand Awareness and Reputation Management through Social Media

Social media also plays a pivotal role in brand awareness. Through consistent content production and social engagement, corporations can imprint their brand identity on the audience's minds. Platforms like Instagram and Facebook allow businesses to showcase their values, ethos, and offerings prominently, effectively shaping their brand persona.

In addition, social media provides businesses with an invaluable tool for managing their reputation. Being proactive and responding promptly to customer feedback illustrates a company's commitment to customer satisfaction, which boosts credibility and trustworthiness. Plus, it aids in damage control during crisis situations, enabling corporations to maintain their brand image intact.

2.4. Tapping into Social Media Analytics for Business Growth

The deceptively playful nature of social media belies its functionality as a data-heavy tool. Platforms come equipped with analytical features that provide insightful consumer data, from demographic details to behavioural patterns. This data serves as feedback for the businesses, fuelling their marketing strategies and guiding their decision-making processes.

Furthermore, through social listening, businesses can monitor conversations around their brand or industry, thus equipping themselves with insights to stay ahead of competition and spot trends early on.

2.5. Social Media as a Sales and Lead Generation Tool

Finally, social media functions as an effective sales and lead generation conduit. By strategically sprinkling calls-to-action in their posts, businesses can guide users through the sales funnel. Platforms like Instagram and Pinterest now offer 'shoppable posts', blurring the line between social and commercial platforms.

Businesses, especially those in the e-commerce sector, can leverage this feature to shorten the customer's journey to purchase, boosting conversions and sales. This feature, coupled with social media advertising options, tangibly impacts a corporation's bottom line, attesting to the power social media wields over business.

In conclusion, social media's power in business is both undeniable and essential to harness. As the lines between the digital and physical world continue to blur, we're reminded: not being present on social media doesn't make a brand invisible, but rather irrelevant. It's incumbent upon corporations to understand and utilize these platforms strategically to carve their digital identity and ensure their success in the burgeoning digital marketplace.

Chapter 3. Assessing Your Current Corporate Social Media Presence

In the world of digital marketing, the first crucial step towards success is acknowledging that every corporate entity has a default presence on social media whether they're actively participating in it or not. The way your brand is mentioned, talked about, and perceived in the bustling Internet landscape paints a panoramic picture of your current corporate social media presence. Thus, assessing this existing presence can prove to be an invaluable exercise in identifying the strengths, weaknesses, opportunities, and potential pitfalls facing your business in the realm of social media.

3.1. Cutting Through the Social Noise: Clear Understanding is Key

To cut through the clamor of the social media sphere, seek to understand not just your brand's presence, but also the rich and varied tapestry in which it is embedded. Start by compiling a list of social media platforms where your brand is mentioned or has an active presence. Separate platforms into tiers based on relevance to your business model, target audience, and strategic goals. Facebook, Twitter, LinkedIn, Instagram, YouTube, TikTok, Pinterest, and SnapChat among others might be potential contenders.

For each platform, gather data on a number of followers, engagement rates (likes, shares, comments), types of content shared, posting frequency, and any distinctive patterns or trends. Visually representing this data using graphs or tables can help illuminate any striking patterns or outliers worth closer exploration.

3.2. Your Brand's Digital Footprint: Deciphering the Social Media Landscape

Having located your brand on various platforms, carry out an in-depth review of your business' online identity. Focus on aspects like the tone and language of the content, visual elements such as logos, color scheme, header and profile images, and overall aesthetic of your feed. The aim is to understand how you are visually and textually representing your brand at present and whether it aligns with the overall brand image and values you want to project.

Scrutinize the engagement aspect: which types of posts garner attention and provoke interaction? What chronology does your social media activity follow? Is it consistent? Thoroughly appraise past campaigns for their performance and reception. Use in-platform analytics tools, like Facebook Insights and Twitter Analytics, for granular metrics like reach, impressions, and engagement.

3.3. Social Listening: What are They Saying About You?

Social listening refers to tracking brand mentions and relevant conversations across social media platforms and the web at large. Important aspects to consider include the sentiment behind the mentions (positive, neutral, negative), the volume of these mentions, and any prevalent themes or recurring topics in these conversations. There are many third-party tools, like Hootsuite, Brandwatch, and Mention, that can automate this process and provide in-depth analytics.

Frequency distributions, word clouds or sentiment charts can prove helpful in understanding public perception and sentiment towards your brand, and identify potential crises before they spiral out of control. By doing so, you're also benchmarking these scores – which would be useful to gauge the progress you make in the future after implementing the strategies discussed further in this report.

3.4. Digital SWOT Analysis for Your Social Media Presence

Based on these assessments, draw up a tailored SWOT analysis – Strengths, Weaknesses, Opportunities and Threats – of your corporate social media presence. In the matrix, strengths could include high levels of engagement or a unique tone of voice. Weaknesses might be inconsistent posting schedules or low follower count. Opportunities could encompass untapped potential on a trending social media platform, or proactively addressing a common customer complaint that often pops up in social listening. Threats might involve negative PR or rising competition.

Remember, this exercise is an opportunity for introspection and improvement – celebrate strengths, identify weak links, tap into hidden opportunities, and plan ahead for possible threats.

3.5. The Role of Competitive Analysis

No assessment is complete without examining your presence in relation to key competitors. Identify 3-5 key competitors and repeat the steps above to create a snapshot of their social media presence. Use this comparative analysis to benchmark your results and direct your improvement efforts.

Assessing your current social media presence might seem like a daunting exercise at first, especially given the scope and pace of the digital world. However, it's a lot like navigating through a forest -

with the right map (this report), compass (methodical approach), and binoculars (appropriate tools), you're well-equipped to chart the course to your destination: a compelling, engaging, and impactful corporate social media presence.

Chapter 4. Defining Your Brand Voice for Social Media

In an era of intense digital noise and overwhelming content flows, defining a unique and resonant brand voice for your social media is an instrumental piece of your corporate identity puzzle. This chapter, essentially a deep dive into the task of shaping your brand voice, seeks to provide a meticulous guide for corporate businesses intending to tether their brand identity firmly on social media platforms.

4.1. Constructing Your Corporate Identity

Before you venture into the creating a distinct brand voice for your social media platforms, it is essential, to begin with, a solid grasp of your corporate identity. Understanding your business's ethos, objectives, and unique selling points form the base for defining your brand voice. It's also crucial to properly understand your corporate culture, mission statements, and overall image as perceived by the public. Often, corporate identity is the anchor that helps the brand voice remain steady amidst the turbulent waves of social media trends.

4.2. Understanding and Embodying Your Brand Personality

The essence of carving your brand voice lies in understanding and articulating your brand personality. This resonates directly with the ethos of your corporation and diversity of your customer base. Consider your brand as a person. What would it sound like? Is it serious, quirky, professional, fun-loving, empathetic, analytical, authoritative, or adventurous? The key is ensuring that your brand personality fits smartly with your industry type and the demographic you're targeting.

4.3. The Semantic Landscape

Once you have a clear understanding of your brand personality, you need to determine how it manifests in day-to-day communication. This implementation pivots around linguistic and semantic choices. From the words and phrases you choose to the tone and style of your messaging, your brand voice is woven into every single interaction on social media. Be mindful of the language that is likely to resonate with your audience. Too formal, too casual, too verbose, or too terse–each comes with its pros and cons. Balance is essential.

4.4. Consistency is Key

In the realm of social media, where trends rise and fall within hours, consistency may seem like an unattainable ideal. However, in the context of your brand voice, continuity is undeniably crucial. Not just across different social media platforms, but consistency should also be maintained between your online and offline presence. Consistency carves out recognition and loyalty, allowing your audience to become familiar with your brand voice and anticipate your messaging.

4.5. Developing a Social Media Style Guide

To maintain consistency and ensure understanding across your team, a social media style guide can be extremely beneficial. The social media style guide should include your brand's character/persona, tonality, the do's and don'ts of language, preferred and non-preferred terminology, the syntax of messaging, and responses to potential scenarios. Case studies demonstrating good and bad examples of your brand voice can be particularly useful. Remember that this is a living document and should be regularly updated to keep pace with your company's growth and evolution.

4.6. Audience Engagement and Feedback Incorporation

Finally, once you have defined and implemented your brand voice, it's time to check how well it's performing. Continuously monitoring how your audience interacts with your brand voice is an excellent thermometer to gauge its temperature. Negative feedback is not an indication to revamp your entire brand voice instantaneously, but it is a sign that changes should be made. Regularly assess and adapt your brand voice based on audience feedback, industry changes, and the evolution of your own corporate values and objectives.

Remember that defining your brand voice for social media is not a one-time activity. It is a continuous process, an unending dialogue between your brand and your audience. Remain flexible and adaptable, and your brand voice will continue to grow and resonate powerfully amidst the cacophony of the digital world, enabling your brand to stand tall in the crowded landscape of social media.

Chapter 5. Embracing the Power of Content: Strategy and Creation

The digital realm is an engine that thrives on content. Like a lifeblood permeating through the digital ecosystem, content has the power to attract, engage, enlighten, and inspire audiences, leading to increased brand recognition, customer loyalty, and ultimately, business growth. Equipped with a potent mix of creativity and strategic planning, a compelling content strategy can spell the difference between being just another company online and a powerful branding force, creating ripples across your industry.

5.1. The Power of Content in the Digital Sphere

Content in the digital context transcends traditional boundaries and includes any piece of information, whether textual or visual, that serves a specific purpose. This could range from blogs and articles to infographics, podcasts, webinars, and social media posts—each presenting unique opportunities for engagement. High-quality content that resonates with audiences acts as social currency, allowing businesses to connect, educate, entertain, and sustain conversations with their target market in countless ways.

5.2. Crafting a Bespoke Content Strategy

Crafting an effective content strategy is similar to planning a journey. It requires a meticulously drafted roadmap, outlining where you are, where you hope to be, and how to get there. First, understand your audience. In-depth demographic and psychographic analysis will provide deeper insights into what type of content genuinely resonates with your target market. Second, define your content goals. Are you looking to build brand awareness, boost customer engagement, or perhaps drive more conversions? Clear objectives enable focused and purposeful content creation. Finally, consider the channels you wish to use. Consider each platform's nuances and its user demographics to tailor your strategy successfully.

5.3. Creating Magnetic Content

Successful content creation is an art backed by data. On the one hand, it involves a touch of creativity to make your content stand out. On the other, it requires a solid understanding of user behavior, engagement metrics, and SEO principles to ensure your creative efforts do not go unnoticed. Keywords, backlinks, meta descriptions, and more, all play a critical role in optimizing your content for visibility. However, it isn't just about appeasing algorithms but also creating meaningful dialogues with your audiences through relatable and impactful content.

5.4. Content Types and Their Power

Different content types cater to various stages of the buyer's journey and the ever-changing customer moods. Blog posts and articles are excellent tools to provide value and build thought leadership. Infographics and video content are often more engaging and shareable, widening your reach. Case studies and whitepapers instill confidence, while podcasts provide a more intimate way of sharing insights. Understanding the power of each content type, their proclivity to specific platforms, and knowing when to fuse various elements can make your content strategy truly versatile.

5.5. The Role of Consistency and Adaptability

Consistency is the thread that binds your narrative together across different platforms and content types. It contributes to a coherent brand image, imbued with relevance and authenticity. Yet, amidst this consistency, it is equally critical to stay adaptable and responsive to current trends, user feedback, and algorithmic changes. This fluidity ensures your content remains fresh, relevant, and ready to seize unexpected opportunities.

5.6. Looking Beyond Creation: Distribution and Promotion

Content creation is only half the battle. A meticulously planned distribution strategy ensures your content reaches the intended audience. Diversifying distribution channels, promoting content at optimal times and leveraging shareability are all pivotal. Amplify your reach through paid promotions, collaborative content, guest posting, and more, turning your content into a powerful beacon attracting users toward your brand.

5.7. The Cycle of Evaluation and Optimization

No content strategy can remain stagnant. Embrace an iterative process of evaluation and optimization. Harness the power of analytics to extract valuable data on user interaction, engagement metrics, bounce rates, and more. These insights serve not just to gauge the success of your content but also to inform future strategy, creating a cycle of continuous improvement and growth.

From conception to execution, nurturing to optimization, embracing the power of content is no small task. Yet, the potential return on investment—a resonant brand image, a loyal customer base, and an amplified digital presence—is undoubtedly worth the effort. So, let's raise the curtain on your content journey, seize the tools of strategy and creation, and sculpt a social media presence that truly makes waves. The dawn of your digital metamorphosis begins here.

Chapter 6. Utilizing Influencers: Building Relationships for Impact

The world of social media thrives on influence. Shared ideas, trending topics, viral videos, and hashtags catapult ordinary users into the spotlight, driving engagement and shaping public discourse. For businesses aspiring to a solid online presence, working with influencers can be a transformative strategy. Influencers are not just prominent figures circulating in the course of social media; they also bring along impassioned communities who trust and admire them. Contracting in with the right influencer can amp up your brand's visibility, credibility, and ultimately, your bottom line.

6.1. The Power and Impact of Using Influencers

Utilizing influencers is not a novel idea. Brands have been harnessing the power of notable people to advertise their products for a long time—think of celebrity endorsements. But in the realm of social media, the concept of influence expands, encompassing more than just the well-known names. Here, influencers could be industry thought leaders, trending YouTube vloggers, high-followed Instagrammers, micro-influencers with a compact but engaged followership, and even TikTok sensations creating viral content. Each type of influencer brings a unique flavor to your brand's online identity and holds the potential to resonate differently with your audience.

Influencer collaborations may help to authenticate your brand's narrative since users tend to trust peer recommendations more than advertisements. A well-executed influencer collaboration can draw millions of eyes to your products without the perception of being a hard sell. Engagement soars, and so do conversions. Marketers who were quick to adopt influencer collaborations report seeing tremendous ROIs, which only underlines the immense potential it holds for your brand.

6.2. Identifying the Right Influencers

Choosing the correct influencer to partner with is a crucial first step in your brand's influencer marketing journey. Considering visibility, reputation, followership size, and aesthetics is essential, but it doesn't stop there.

Your chosen influencer should align with your brand values, be that commitment towards sustainability, a focus on tech innovation, or a cause close to your company's heart. This alignment will ensure coherence in your brand messaging, creating a stronger brand narrative across media.

Do your research – is the influencer respected and trusted in their community? Do they produce high-quality content? What's their follower to engagement ratio? Are their followers your target demographic?

Cross-analysis of these metrics will guide you towards influencers who are not just popular, but who can truly deliver results for your brand.

6.3. Building Meaningful Relationships

After identifying aligned influencers, the process of building relationships with them commences. This isn't transactional, but an investment — resembling a partnership more than a one-off engagement.

Mutual respect and understanding should pepper your communication. Building a rapport with your influencers can lead to successful collaborations. Regular check-ins, respecting their creative process, and providing them with constructive feedback are excellent steps towards building a strong relationship.

Instead of overly prescriptive guidelines, allow influencers the creative freedom to present your product authentically in their style. Remember, their followers value their unique voice, and sticking to it increases the chance of your collaboration resonating with them.

6.4. Measuring the Impact of Your Influencer Partnerships

After your influencers have published their branded content, the next undertaking is to assess the impact of this partnership. This involves tracking engagement metrics to comprehend the effectiveness of the campaign.

Key metrics include impressions, likes, shares, comments, conversions, and more, depending on your objectives. For instance, if your goal is enhancing brand awareness, excellent metrics would be shares and impressions. If it's to drive sales, track conversions and click-through-rates.

It's crucial to remember that these metrics should be assessed in the context of your original goals and objectives. For tracking effectively, using an analytics tool or a comprehensive influencer marketing platform can prove beneficial.

6.5. Navigating Challenges in Influencer Marketing

Like any digital marketing strategy, influencer marketing is not without its pitfalls. From influencer fraud, where users artificially inflate their followership, to controversies surrounding the influencer potentially damaging your brand, the risks are tangible. A robust vetting process and a strong crisis management plan can help navigate these challenges, protecting your brand and enhancing the benefits of your influencer partnerships.

6.6. Looking Ahead: Influencer Marketing in the Future

While trends will undoubtedly continue to shift in the social media sphere, influencer marketing appears poised to remain a juggernaut. As user habits evolve, so too will the ways in which influencers reach and engage them. With the advent of technologies like AI and virtual reality, influencers could branch out into new realms and platforms, creating fresh opportunities for brands to connect with their audiences.

As we step into the future, maintaining authentic, strategic influencer relationships will continue to be key. By understanding your brand values, identifying influencers that align with these, and focusing on building enduring partnerships, your brand can effectively navigate the evolving landscape of influencer marketing in social media. After all, it is not just about utilizing influencers—it's about building relationships for impact.

Chapter 7. Engaging the Audience: The Art of Communication in Social Media

In the ever-evolving realm of social media, the art of audience engagement serves as an essential toolkit that enables organizations to establish and maintain valuable relationships with their diverse audience. This intricate art form combines several key elements, including the crafting of resonant messages, deep understanding of platform algorithms, and the deployment of strategic communication techniques.

7.1. Foundational Pillars of Audience Engagement

Audience engagement is comprised of three foundational pillars: Content Relevance, Audience Interactivity, and Continuous Evolution. Let's delve deeper into each of these pillars.

1. Content Relevance: Ensuring the relevance of your content is key to capturing and retaining audience attention. Your messaging should resonate with your audience's interests, values, and needs. Keep in mind that your audience's preferences are diverse and continuously vary. For instance, a younger demographic might prefer light-hearted, visual-based content such as memes or GIFs, while a professional audience may find value-adding, insightful articles or industry updates more appealing. The underlying principle of content relevance is an in-depth understanding of your audience — their preferences, behaviors, and needs.

2. Audience Interactivity: The beauty of social media lies in its interactivity. Encourage user interaction by taking initiatives like inviting comments, conducting polls, organizing live Q&A sessions, or launching user-generated content campaigns. Social media platforms tend to prioritize content that sparks interaction, meaning posts that solicit robust responses from users often achieve increased visibility. This increased visibility, in turn, can significantly augment your brand's reach and influence.

3. Continuous Evolution: Social media trends are notoriously fleeting, shifting like the tides. It necessitates a mindset of continuous evolution. Stay abreast of the latest trends on different platforms to ensure your content remains fresh, attractive, and engaging. This may mean adopting the latest content formats (like Instagram Reels or LinkedIn Stories), participating in viral challenges, or integrating trending keywords or hashtags into your posts. Remember, stagnation is the enemy of engagement in the vibrant ecosystem of social media.

7.2. Communication Strategies That Foster Engagement

Now that we've established a robust foundation, let's contemplate some strategic methodologies that can amplify your audience engagement levels.

User-Persona Targeting

Understanding who your audience is critical. Creating user personas can be a valuable exercise in understanding the different segments of your audience comprehensively. User personas reflect the characteristics of your target audience, such as demographics, interests, behaviors, and motivations. Targeting these personas with tailored content can heighten their connection with your brand and increase your content's engagement rate.

Ticks of Timing

In the digital milieu, timing is everything. Posting when your audience is most active maximizes your content's visibility and traction. Tools like Native Analytics on platforms like Facebook and Instagram, or third-party tools like Hootsuite and Sprout Social, can provide insights into when your audience is most active.

Conversations over Campaigns

In the modern era, people crave authentic communication more than canned campaigns. Facilitate genuine conversations by asking questions, prompting discussions, or discussing trending topics. Making your brand feel more 'human' can significantly enhance engagement.

Storytelling and Emotion

Storytelling can be a powerful tool for promoting audience engagement. Well-crafted narratives have the power to captivate audiences, hold their attention, and inspire action. Incorporate stories into your social content, whether it's the story of your brand, customer testimonials, or behind-the-scenes tales about your team. When these stories inspire emotion – be it joy, surprise, empathy, or excitement – they are likely to result in higher audience engagement.

Compelling Content Formats

Embrace the diversity of content formats available on different platforms - text updates, images, videos, live streams, infographics, podcasts, and more. Video content, in particular, has proven to drive high engagement rates across various social platforms.

7.3. Mastering Digital Empathy: The Ultimate Engagement Tool

In this digital age, where real human contact is often replaced by online interactions, demonstrating empathy towards your audience can create a profound connection. Digital empathy refers to the ability to understand and respect the feelings, needs, and perspectives of your audience in the online realm. By acknowledging your audience's concerns, appreciating their contributions, celebrating their successes, and offering support in times of difficulty, you foster a sense of community and trust that motivates further interactions and deepens audience engagement.

Incorporating these concepts and principles into your social media strategy can dramatically elevate your brand's engagement rates. Remember, the realm of social media is an ongoing journey, filled with constant learning, unlearning, and relearning. Continue to experiment with different approaches, evaluate the results, and adapt accordingly. Stay curious, stay open-minded, and above all, stay engaging.

Chapter 8. Mastering Social Media Platforms: A Guide to Facebook, Twitter, LinkedIn, and More

In the dynamic digital space we inhabit, mastering various social media platforms is akin to learning different languages, each with its own culture, code of conduct, and communication norms. As a business, it becomes critical to comprehend the nuances of these platforms, as well as their respective strengths and characteristics, to ensure that your message is effectively and influentially communicated to your intended audience.

8.1. Understanding Facebook for Business

Facebook, with its over 2.8 billion active users, offers a vast sea of potentials and possibilities for businesses globally. You can tap into its numerous features like personal profiles for employees, business pages for companies and products, and groups for communities centered around common interests and objectives.

Firstly, creating a Facebook Business Page provides your company with an official presence on the platform. It not only aids visibility but also allows for interaction with a global customer base. However, mere existence on the platform won't suffice. You need to optimally engage with your audience via regular posts, news updates, product launches, behind-the-scenes, and running various marketing campaigns.

On Facebook, the algorithms prioritize posts that stimulate

conversation and meaningful interactions between people. Hence, it is essential to craft content that triggers engaging discussions and shares. The timing of your posts also plays a pivotal role; study your analytics to identify when your audience is most active.

One of the essential digital marketing tools embedded in Facebook is Facebook Ads Manager. This platform allows businesses to target specific audience demographics, thereby enhancing the reach and effectiveness of promotional campaigns. Companies can also leverage Facebook Insights for comprehensive analytical data to fine-tune their strategies continually.

8.2. Navigating Twitter for Business

Twitter, with its 192 million daily active users, is a critical platform for real-time information and conversations. It promotes direct communication between businesses and consumers, making it a powerful tool for customer interaction and service.

Establishing an impactful presence on Twitter involves more than broadcasting your updates; you must also converse, listen, and engage with your audience. Timely responses, authentic communication, and transparency are essential in establishing trust and reputation on this platform.

Twitter is also a fertile ground for using hashtags effectively – they can increase the visibility of your tweets, follow industry trends, or jump into existing dialogues. The platform also allows you to promote your tweets or run ad campaigns targeted towards specific audience metrics. Do not forget the power of analytics on Twitter, which provides detailed statistical insight to help tailor your engagement strategies.

8.3. Harnessing LinkedIn for Business

LinkedIn, a professional networking platform with over 740 million members, is an indispensable tool for B2B companies. It provides opportunities not just for recruitment but also for brand promotion, thought leadership, and networking.

Having a detailed, up-to-date, and active LinkedIn Company Page can significantly enhance your credibility. It allows you the opportunity to showcase your brand image, projects, values, and culture. Participating meaningfully in LinkedIn Groups or creating bespoke groups can also provide a valuable industry connection and engagement.

LinkedIn's Content Suggestions tool provides customized content ideas based on your industry and audience. The platform's advertising opportunities are also rewarding, especially for B2B marketing. LinkedIn's analytics afford businesses a deep dive into their reach, engagement, and follower demographics to refine their strategy.

To sum up, mastering social media platforms and aligning them with your business goals necessitates a comprehensive understanding of the platforms' potentials and an idiosyncratic approach to harnessing them. Remember, the key lies not in speaking the loudest but in ensuring every word matters, resonates, and is ultimately valued by your potential and existing customers. As we continue to traverse this digital cosmos together, the digital imprint you leave must gleam with engagement, thought leadership, authenticity, and value.

Chapter 9. Monitoring, Measuring, and Adapting: The Role of Analytics in Corporate Social Media

In the curlicues of digital activity, you will find that the world of corporate social media is duplicitous. On one side, it opens up myriad opportunities to engage with customers and foster brand communities. On the other side, it presents an interesting challenge: how to track the success of these endeavours? Here's where analytics steps in as a warder, guiding your brand in its quest to understand, interact with, and adapt to the fluctuating rhythms of your social media campaign.

9.1. The Essence of Analytics in Social Media

Making informed decisions is a sine qua non for any business, particularly when it applies to social media. The multiplicity of factors involved - the type of content, posting times, customer reactiveness, successful campaigns, weak areas, emerging trends, and so forth - prove that this isn't an arena for muddled understanding or uncertain navigation. Analytics presents a technicolor perspective by collecting, interpreting, and translating vast amounts of data into actionable insights. It serves as both the cartographer documenting the current terrain and the compass pointing towards future directions.

To say that social media analytics is important would perhaps be an oversimplification; it is crucial. It supports brands in a variety of ways, from determining overall business strategy to identifying valuable customer segments, to gauging the impact and effectiveness of marketing campaigns. A strong analytics foundation can drastically reduce trial and error, provide an in-depth understanding of your audience, and allow you to make more accurate predictions.

9.2. Differentiating and Understanding Key Metrics

Modern social media platforms provide a plethora of metrics. Thankfully, they can be roughly categorized under four primary types: engagement, reach, leads, and conversions. All your social media activities can be measured against these performance indicators.

1. **Engagement**: This includes likes, comments, shares, mentions, saves, direct messages, among others. It essentially represents the level of interaction your content has inspired. As a rule of thumb, higher engagement often translates to a well-received content strategy.

2. **Reach**: Reach shows the number of unique users exposed to your content. While high reach is an indicator of broad exposure, it does not necessarily equal engagement.

3. **Leads**: A lead refers to any potential customer who shows an interest in your brand by partaking in actions like filling an online form or subscribing to a newsletter.

4. **Conversions**: Conversions refer to leads that turned into customers. By tracking conversions, you can see how effectively your social media efforts are contributing to sales.

Delineating these categories and recognizing their unique roles simplifies the daunting task of analytics. More so, it helps in creating platform-specific strategies.

9.3. Utilizing Social Media Analytics Tools

To efficiently work with social media analytics, you need to wield the right tools. Luckily, there's a wide array of resources available which cater to a spectrum of needs and levels of expertise.

For beginners, native analytics tools offered by platforms such as Twitter Analytics, Facebook Insights, and LinkedIn Analytics are a great starting point. These conventional tools provide a comprehensive analysis of your social media performance right from within the platform, eliminating the need for separate software or highly specialized knowledge.

For those seeking more in-depth insights, third-party tools like Sprout Social, Hootsuite, and Buffer offer advanced analytics capabilities. Not only do these tools provide detailed statistics on performance metrics, but they also allow cross-platform analysis, competitor benchmarking, and automated report generation – a feature that will prove invaluable when sharing results with stakeholders.

9.4. Tailoring Your Strategy with Insights

Learning to adapt your strategy swiftly based on insights is the culmination point of analytics. By leveraging data, you can capitalize on what works and jettison what doesn't, thus reinventing your social media approach, one insight at a time.

For instance, if your Twitter posts get more engagement in the evenings, consider scheduling more posts for that time frame. On the other hand, if LinkedIn posts show more reach but lesser conversions, you might want to work on enhancing your call-to-actions or post-click landing pages for that platform.

Never underestimate the power of constant iteration. While it may seem a tedious process, it is in these incremental adaptations and improvements that the true strength of an insightful social media strategy lies.

9.5. Conclusion: The Dance of Monitoring, Measuring, and Adapting

Navigating the social media maze can seem like a mammoth task, but equipped with analytical tools and insights, you are more than capable of turning what appears like a chaotic dance into a well-choreographed ballet. Flexibility is the cornerstone of a successful social media strategy, and analytics endorses just that. By monitoring the ebb and flow of social media interactions, measuring performance through critical metrics, and adapting strategies in line with insights garnered, you can march towards assured social media success. Like the watchful eyes of a seasoned choreographer, let analytics guide your brand in its dance in the sunlit stage of social media.

Chapter 10. Dealing with Crisis: Damage Control in the Digital World

In the rapidly evolving landscape of social media, handling crises is an essential skillset. The implications of a poorly managed corporate crisis can range from public backlash to a significant dip in market value. As such, we begin this chapter by exploring the factors that lead to digital crises, before moving on to discuss pragmatic strategies for effective damage control.

10.1. Understanding the Nature of Digital Crises

A digital crisis can be likened to a wildfire in the cyber forest—it starts small but can quickly escalate into a colossal disaster if not addressed promptly and adequately. Information travels at lightning speed on the internet, and a small, seemingly harmless incident can snowball into a brand disaster virtually overnight.

Whether it's a scandalous tweet, an insensitive advertisement, a data breach, or a customer service mishap, crises can arise from a multitude of sources. Some can be prevented, while others are inevitable. Understanding the nature of these crises is the first step to formulating an effective response strategy.

10.2. Building a Crisis Management Plan

In dealing with a crisis, it is essential to have a pre-existing crisis management plan. This plan should include a comprehensive risk assessment, a system for rapid response, and guidelines for communication.

At this point, we must stress the importance of recognizing a crisis in the earliest stages. Develop intuitive systems that track mentions, customer feedback, and other external signals. Swift detection is half the battle; it presents an opportunity for a timely intervention before the crisis spirals out of control.

The plan should also highlight your corporate communication style. Ensure that your responses maintain a consistent tone and adhere to your brand values, irrespective of the intensity or complexity of the crisis at hand.

10.3. Leveraging Social Media for Crisis Management

Intrinsically, social media platforms offer immense benefits for crisis management. Their real-time nature can help facilitate immediate communication with stakeholders and the public at large. Brands can use social media to quickly distribute official statements, apologize if necessary, and keep the audience updated on resolution progress.

However, communicating through social media should be handled delicely. Avoid sounding robotic or insincere. Show empathy and understanding. Importantly, engage. Address queries, alleviate concerns, and most crucially, listen. Here, proactiveness goes a long way in controlling damage and rebuilding trust.

10.4. Monitoring and Analyzing the Crisis

The true measure of an effective crisis management strategy is not merely how quickly the issue got resolved, but also how well the crisis was understood and what lessons were learned.

For this purpose, it is important to use social media analytics. Monitor conversations and sentiment around your brand during and after the crisis. Recognize patterns, understand public response, and identify key influencers who could either propagate the crisis or assist in its resolution.

Notably, the learnings from the crisis analysis should feed into your crisis management plan. Optimize and iterate, so your system grows more robust with each incident.

10.5. Devising a Recovery Strategy

Surviving a social media crisis isn't just about weathering the storm; it's about coming out stronger on the other side. Brands should embrace the opportunity to learn from their mistakes, regain public favor, and strengthen their online reputation.

An effective recovery strategy starts with a sincere apology but doesn't end there. Companies should demonstrate their commitment to change by outlining clear steps to prevent similar situations in the future. The audience values transparency, and proactive change can be a potent reputational recovery tool.

To sum up, properly dealing with a crisis in the digital world is a combination of preparation, swift action, thoughtful communication, deep analysis, and diligent recovery. Remember, the aim is not just to 'save face,' but to transform a potential disaster into a learning opportunity, ultimately strengthening the brand's corporate social media presence. With the tools and strategies outlined in this chapter, you are better equipped to navigate any digital storm that may come your way.

Chapter 11. Looking Ahead: The Future of Corporate Social Media Presence

In an era of relentless digital evolution, the multifaceted landscape of Corporate Social Media Presence is in a state of constant flux. As businesses strive to carve out their digital spaces, staying ahead of the curve is paramount. This chapter is designed to focus a lens on the foreseeable future, drawing on expert opinion, industry trends, and foresight, to help your brand navigate the uncharted waters of the future social media landscape.

11.1. The Continuing Rise of Visual Content

As the popular adage goes: "A picture's worth a thousand words," and it has never been more valid than in today's social media realm. The surging popularity of platforms like Instagram, TikTok, and Pinterest point to the increasingly visual nature of online content consumption. Brands are expected to creatively harness the power of visual storytelling to captivate their audiences. This includes high-quality images, infographics, short and intuitive videos, animations, virtual tours, and more.

Emerging technologies like Augmented and Virtual Reality are poised to further enhance visual content, providing immersive experiences that can create a deeper connection between brands and their customers. By actively integrating these technologies into their social media strategy, companies can unlock innovative avenues for showcasing their products or services, thereby reinforcing their Corporate Social Media Presence.

11.2. The Proliferation of Ephemeral Content

Ephemeral content – content that is only accessible for a short duration – has been enjoying an unprecedented surge in popularity. Users are increasingly enthralled by the fleeting, yet highly engaging nature of Snapchat Stories, Instagram Stories, Facebook Stories, and Fleets on Twitter. The paradoxical charm of such short-lived content lies in its spontaneous, genuine and compelling qualities, creating a sense of urgency and exclusivity.

In the rapidly changing scenario, it is anticipated that brands will actively employ ephemeral content as a part of their social media strategy. This tactic can prove effective in maintaining regular customer interaction, promoting timely offers, or simply keeping your brand at the top of the audience's feed. As the trend deepens, companies will need to master the balance between quality and quantity to truly leverage ephemeral content for their advantage.

11.3. User-Generated Content and Co-Creation

User-Generated Content (UGC), already a powerful tool in the corporate social media strategy, will continue to gain importance in the future. UGC, such as reviews, testimonials, or user-created videos and photos, infuses a brand's image with authenticity and credibility. This content plays a vital role in shaping purchasing decisions and building long-term customer loyalty.

Companies are likely to delve deeper into co-creating content with their audience in the future. This strategy invites consumers to be active contributors, thereby fostering a stronger sense of community and engagement around the brand. By creatively promoting UGC and co-creation, companies can foster brand advocacy, deepen customer relationships, and strengthen their social media presence.

11.4. The Advent of Social Commerce

Social Commerce, the process of selling products directly on social media platforms, is on the rise. As platforms like Facebook, Instagram, and Pinterest continue to refine their shopping features, consumers are increasingly turning to social media for a one-stop shopping experience. This trend offers a seamless blend of online shopping and social media surfing, providing brands an opportunity to directly convert social media engagement into sales.

The future of Corporate Social Media Presence is likely to see a wider adoption of this strategy, as more brands leverage the appeal of 'Buy Now' buttons or shoppable posts. By unifying their social media and e-commerce strategies, brands can both enhance the customer shopping experience and augment their online presence.

11.5. The Emergence of AI and Chatbots

Artificial Intelligence (AI) and chatbots continue to revolutionize the way brands interact with their customers on social media. Thanks to advancements in machine learning, chatbots are becoming ever more sophisticated, capable of handling complex customer queries and providing personalized responses in real-time.

AI capabilities extend beyond just chatbots, offering valuable insights about customer behavior and preferences by analyzing vast amounts of social media data. These insights can then be used to fine-tune a brand's social media strategy, thus ensuring it remains relevant and engaging. Given these benefits, it is foreseeable that AI and chatbots will play an integral part in shaping Corporate Social Media Presence in the future.

11.6. The Reinforcement of Privacy and Transparency

In light of the recent spate of data privacy breaches, consumers are growing more concerned about the safety of their data. As a result, they increasingly expect brands to uphold stringent data privacy standards and to be transparent in their data use policies. Brands that can successfully demonstrate their commitment to data protection are likely to gain customer trust and loyalty.

Future Corporate Social Media Presence will need to take these consumer concerns seriously, integrating effective data protection measures and clearly communicating these to their users. Striking the right balance between leveraging consumer data for personalized marketing and respecting user privacy will be critical in shaping a brand's social media strategy and its presence in the digital domain.

Looking ahead, the future of Corporate Social Media Presence seems to be characterized by increased personalization, transparency, and user participation, coalescing through converging trends and cutting-edge technologies. In this scenario, brands must stay agile, continually updating their social media strategies with an eye on the horizon and open minds for innovation. With a meticulous approach and a foresighted strategy, companies can ensure that they not only adapt to changing landscapes but also shape their trajectories in the dynamically evolving ecosphere of social media.

www.ingramcontent.com/pod-product-compliance
Lightning Source LLC
Chambersburg PA
CBHW071049260726
48661CB00007B/3224